T0158057

My Hands
Selected Poetry from a Nurse

Paul Phelps

Inspiring Voices books may be ordered through booksellers or by contacting:

Inspiring Voices
1663 Liberty Drive
Bloomington, IN 47403
www.inspiringvoices.com
1 (866) 697-5313

ISBN: 978-1-4624-0843-6 (sc)
ISBN: 978-1-4624-0844-3 (e)

Library of Congress Control Number: 2013921911

Printed in the United States of America.

Inspiring Voices rev. date: 11/26/2013

Contents

We Care

We do our job because we care.
We care about you, your family, and your friends.
We have cultivated our craft
to be able to care for you
when you are at your most vulnerable,
when you are too sick to care for yourself,
when you need our medicine, our machines,
when you can't breathe on your own,
when you can't feed yourself,
when you can't get out of bed
or even clean up after yourself.
We will bathe you, change your sheets.
We will feed you and bring you warm blankets.
We will wipe your brow, hold your hand.
We will pray for you and with you.
We will work for you.
That's why we are here.
That's why we are nurses.
We do it all for you.

Another Soul

We can keep a body alive—almost forever—
but can our technology keep the spirit alive?
We have machines to keep you breathing,
medicine to keep your heart beating.
We can feed you through an IV line
or through a tube into your stomach.
We can put in catheters to catch your urine
and tubes to catch your bowel movements.
But where do we draw the line?
When is enough enough?
We wait for the family to make the decision.
We have *care conferences* to discuss
their loved one, the prognosis, the medical condition.
We call their clergy or our chaplain.
Good-byes are said, tears fall, prayers whispered,
and the machines are turned off.
Silence envelops the room,
broken by soft cries and sobs.
Peace reigns at last,
and another soul leaves our ICU.

My Hands

My hands are my strength.
They reach out to comfort the sick.
They help to raise the weak.
My hands bring help to ease your pain,
medicine to heal your body,
a touch to heal your spirit.
At times, my hands bring pain
as they use the needle or IV line.
Yet they comfort the infant in his crib,
wipe the fevered brow,
or simply hold your hand in mine.
They are blessed by our chaplain every year
and by God every day.
You see them mostly covered by rubber gloves,
yet the strength they hold can still be felt,
for my hands are the hands of a nurse.

Ambien

Ambien is my friend,
for it helps to fend
off many late-night calls
and trips down the long halls.

It offers up lots of rest
to patients who are pests,
keeping them sleeping all night long
and by helping to prolong

the quiet of these hours
that are beyond our powers.
As nurses, we come to depend
on Ambien, our little friend.

Haiku 1

The sun has gone down.
Patients are growing confused.
We must prevent falls.

Haiku 2

We work as a team
to keep our patients alive,
we night-shift nurses.

Haiku 3

ICU at night,
the halls are never quiet.
Chaos is normal.

Advice

As a hospital patient,
let me offer some advice.
Do not become complacent,
and always think twice.

Before you annoy your nurse,
you may reap what you sow.
So for better or worse,
just go with the flow.

Remember that we call the shots
and pick the needle's size.
So please think kind thoughts,
and it'll be a pleasant surprise.

Remember that we are in charge,
and look before you leap.
Then we can look forward to discharge
after a good night's sleep.

The Long, Lonely Night

As I work through the long, lonely night,
I am aware of God's ultimate might
to soothe the sick and dry up all the tears.
I watch him answer my silent prayers
as I slip in and out of their rooms silently.
I see them resting so quietly.
I stop for a moment to hold a hand
and offer up my own cowboy brand
of prayer for the souls in my care.
I always know that God can hear.
My thoughts are simple and clear.
I know their guardian angels are near,
and the heavenly Spirit watches on high.
He keeps their souls under his eye,
a place for them in his heart.
In the care I give, his is the lead part.
I care for them here; I'm an ICU nurse.
No matter what happens, for better or worse,
their recovery is only partially in my hands.
It's all a small part of God's greater plans.

The Other Side of the Door

Being a nurse in the ICU,
it's rare to change your point of view.
But I had that rare chance to explore
the view from the other side of the door.
I guess that I became complacent
and then I became the patient.
I came to work on a normal night shift,
when all of a sudden a giant fist
seemingly struck me in the chest.
And, well, you can guess the rest.
A quick trip to the emergency room,
some tests, an EKG, X-ray, then, zoom,
I was whisked away to become another
patient in the ICU, and oh brother,
how my friends greeted me when I arrived.
With friends like these, I'm lucky I survived.
But spending time in a patient's bed
has opened my eyes and cleared my head.
I now know to my very core
how scary it is on the other side of the door.

On Being a Nurse

Being a nurse is really quite a chore.
Sometimes my patients ask for so much more
than I can provide from their doctors' orders.
But now they Google their disorders
and think that they know more than the doctors.
And I find they are really fine actors
when they call all night long for my attention.
They expect me to believe their pain is at a ten,
but their medicine is not due quite then.
They try to pull the wool down over my eyes,
and when I question, they act so darned surprised
that as a nurse I should not believe them,
and I should quickly rush to get the vitamin M,
for morphine is what they seem to crave.
They see me as their own personal slave
who'll run to fulfill their every desire.
But to me, they are singing to the choir.
I have seen all the games that they are trying,
and their bull story I really am not buying.
Then when I finally get tired of their weeping,
I come back in two minutes to find them sleeping.

Burn Unit

A hospital burn unit
is a very special place,
staffed by very special nurses.
The job is uncommonly difficult.
The patients are usually critical,
and the rooms are kept hot.
You have to wear cover gowns,
hair covers, gloves, and masks to enter.
The dressing changes can take hours.
You will sweat out gallons,
it seems like, yet to watch
as your patients improve
and move on with their lives
is one of the greatest rewards
of this special group of nurses.

Code Blue

Code blue, ICU, room 284;
Code blue, ICU, room 284.
The call repeats overhead.
The nurses on the unit have already arrived
before the alarm call can sound.
Our patient has taken a dive.
Our pulses start to bound.
We are working to keep someone alive,
working fast, for we've no seconds to spare.
Ambu bag to inflate lungs deprived.
Chest compressions as long as you can bear.
AED attached to the chest; hold still.
Analyze the rhythm and give a quick shock.
We all know and practice the drill
as the rest of the team starts to flock
into the room to assist in the code.
RT and SWAT nurse, AR, and the doctor—
they have come at our call to share the load.
Intubation and ventilator, the MD is our proctor,
calling out orders for medication and fluid.
One nurse runs the cart; another records.
Two continue compressions; we are all fluent
in this exercise and know the rewards
that come from a successful completion
of our efforts to revive this elderly patient.
It's a small victory that shows our real mission
and reminds us all we can never be complacent.

Deathwatch

Soft voices, hushed words, silent tears
as family and friends draw near,
silently awaiting news that never comes.
Fear grips each footstep, growing closer.
Anxiety waits the opening of the door.
Will this be the final news of their love?
They huddle closer to each other,
seeking strength and courage together
to face this final end, this final good-bye.
Did they pass in peace in their sleep?
Or was pain their final release?
Was there time to prepare, for all to
gather together to share in this final moment?
Or was it quick, with no time to spare
to think or reflect on times past,
the meaning of love and friendship,
and the loss of one so dear?
Final visits, final tears, phone calls, and plans,
and they all finally disappear down the hall.
Another end to another deathwatch.
Another end to a day in the ICU.

Every Age Has Its Duty

Every age has its duty; every age has its call.
The newborn learns to roll and then learns to crawl.
The toddler learns to walk and then begins to run.
The next few years are spent learning how to have fun.
The teen learns to ride a bike and then learns to drive.
The high-schooler learns of college and then learns to strive.
The young adult learns of work and then of love and marriage.
This leads to a home and yard, and then to a baby carriage.
The cycle then continues as they pass on what they've learned
to the next generation, and the tables have been turned.
Our parents are growing old; we've no time to spend.
We're too busy with our lives; it never seems to end.

Float Pool

The life of a float pool nurse
is really quite diverse.
One day you deliver a baby,
and the next night you can maybe
be on the surgical floor
and doing so much more.
And then it's off to the emergency room
for two hours, and then you resume
your tour of the inpatient floors.
But be ready for the tug-of-wars
when one unit is really short-staffed.
You have to manage our craft
to keep from being torn in half.
It can make you cry or laugh,
but it feels great to be in such demand.
Though you seldom work where planned,
one thing I can say with all surety
is that I will always have job security
as long as I don't let my vanity
lead to my insanity.

Alone in His Room

He lies alone in his room,
no pictures on the wall.
No friends come to visit;
no family ever calls.
He had a wife and children.
So many years have past,
but now they have forgotten,
and their father breathes his last.
I give him all the care I can
and sit and hold his hand.
He tells me of his life and times,
of how he loved this land.
He tells me of dreams fulfilled
and some that never came true.
He tells me of the battles fought
when he was a young sailor in blue.
I listen to his tales and share his time.
I hold his hand as he quietly cries.
I wonder about this man in my care,
and I quietly weep as he dies.

I Am a Stranger

I am a stranger, passing in the night,
coming in and going out quietly,
giving a touch, a look, a listen,
checking, monitoring, moving,
as caring and tender as a mother,
as strong and dependable as a father,
as loyal as a brother,
as loving as a sister.
I watch as you sleep.
I cheer as you wake.
I am an arm to lean on when you are weak,
a shoulder to cry on, a hug to be shared,
a touch to show that I care.
I can be the first face you see,
the first hand you hold.
I can be the last voice you hear,
the last touch that lingers as you go.
Neither friend nor enemy,
not lover or spouse,
not family or loved one—
I am your nurse.

I Chose to Be a Nurse

I go to the mountains to a very special place
where I feel that I can talk to God face-to-face.
My life fills me with many questions
that only he can answer by his lessons.
I ask about my role as a nurse.
I feel it's both a blessing and a curse.
I ask to share his infinite wisdom
and about his heavenly kingdom,
and why some are called home so young
while others remain here among
the people he watches here below.
And why does he sometimes bestow
his grace and love to be shared
by those who have never dared
to ask for his blessing or his love
or entrance to his kingdom above?
I know that his grace has strengthened me
and allowed me to be all that I can be.
He has given me the greatest gift of all,
though to many it may seem small.
He has granted me compassion
so I can act as an emblem of his passion
and prove that I followed the right course
when I chose to be a nurse.

I got a note the other night
from the nurse in the ED
to explain and report on our new patient.
I had trouble figuring it out.
This is what it said:
LOL, NAD, NOI, CIB, EMS, DFO@KFC,
HIA, -CT, -LT, OON, NGR, DSS.
I had to call the ED for a translation.
I am an old man and don't speak in text.
This is what I was told:
LOL: Little Old Lady.
NAD: No Apparent Distress
NOI: No Obvious Injury
CIB: Came in By
EMS: Emergency Medical Services
DFO: Done Fell Over
@KFC: At Kentucky Fried Chicken
HIA: Husband in Attendance
-CT: Negative CT Scan
-LT: Negative Lab Test
OON: Observation Overnight
NGR: No Good Reason
DSS: Doctor Says So
I know why we use abbreviations.
It makes for shorter conversations.
But this note takes it to the extreme.
Y I M N RN GOK.

The Dragon

I hear him coming from down the hall,
the hiss and whoosh of his hot breath.
I answer to this, his battle call,
my archenemy, the dragon of death.

This cover gown and the rubber gloves are my armor,
medicine and time the sword and the shield
against the hunger of this snakelike charmer.
I use my strength and skill to make him yield.

The man in the room is unaware of the fight
that we all wage with this terrible beast.
We keep him at bay all day and all night
until his hunger and strength have decreased.

We win the battle this time by our skill
but know the war will only get worse.
We can hold the line, but not stop his will.
To wage this war is my eternal curse

for I am a critical care nurse.

The Art of Nursing

I went to school to become a nurse, and I always have to ponder.
The schools teach the course, and yet I have to wonder.
They teach the science of the trade, but not the art, it's true,
but it's the art by which a nurse is made, and most don't have a clue.
It's found in the little things, like wiping a fevered brow
or treating life's small stings, and taking the time we can allow
to make each patient feel special, like they are your only one,
by slowing down and listening to their story until they are done.
You pause in each and every room to check on how they're doing
and try to wipe away the gloom, and hope your presence is soothing,
and then hurry back to your computer to get your charting done
before they can call out and we start it all again.

Haiku 4

Most nurses are women,
but men are making inroads
in the profession.

Haiku 5

Nursing is a job,
dominated by women,
but men are coming.

The Ghost of the ICU

If I do my job with competence and care,
you will never know that I was there
slipping around quietly and unseen,
moving with confidence and strength
to calm taut nerves and emotions,
to care for the sick and the dying family.
The whole of your world is at an apex,
the future an uncertain void
to be filled over time with sacred
memories of the past, and times
shared with this lost love.
But if I do my job correctly,
I will remain the ghost of the ICU,
the nurse you never knew.

ICU

My ICU patient lies quiet in bed.
The vent hisses and bubbles out its sounds.
The monitor beeps and chirps for attention.
IV pumps work overtime to deliver
the many drugs the doctors have ordered.
Blood pressure drops by the minute.
I titrate the meds and bolus with fluid.
I hang the plasma and pressers.
Her pupils have fixed and dilated.
No gag reflex or cornea response.
Cooling blankets on as the protocol demands,
but will any of this turn her around?
Her fiancé sits in the corner and cries.
Her mother prays and sings songs of her childhood.
Tomorrow the family will gather
to say their good-byes
and care will be withdrawn.
Within the hour
my young patient will die.
This is how my night goes.
I will return tomorrow to the ICU.
I am a nurse; it's what I do.

Twenty–Three Years

Twenty-three years—
    that's all she was given.
Twenty-three years
    till she was called home.
Twenty-three years—
    such a short time here.
Twenty-three years,
yet she thought of others, though her life was so short.
She was a donor of life to others she never knew.
Two will get new kidneys and bid good-bye to machines.
One will get a new liver, a life changed by hers.
One will get new lungs to breathe in new life.
One will get her heart, which was so caring.
Two will get new corneas to see all the good she has done.
Many more will share in her gift through skin to cover their burns
or bones to heal their breaks, yet she was given only
twenty-three years
    to create such a kind spirit,
twenty-three years
    to give so much love,
twenty-three years—
    only twenty-three years.

Haiku 6

Pain is gone at last.
He's standing at heaven's door.
Tears fall silently.

Haiku 7

Fear awakens her.
Her shaking hand do I hold.
Peace returns slowly.

Haiku 8

Ventilators hiss.
The chest rises rhythmically.
Breath of life returns.

Myocardial Infarction

Myocardial infarction or heart attack—
these words really take you aback,
especially when you are a cardiac nurse,
but then I think it could be worse.
These events that happened to me
have increased my understanding and empathy.
They will make me a better nurse and teacher,
more of an advocate, and less of a preacher.
When it comes to my care of my patients' symptoms,
I will see them as people more than victims.
This has helped me better understand
the inconvenience of something you never planned,
the unexpected interruption of a happy life
to one that is now filled with strife,
the changes you will have to make
to your life, and all that is at stake
from the new scary diagnosis,
to the strange words, atherosclerosis,
new medicines, new diets, new exercises,
"stop smoking, stop drinking, and drop five sizes"—
it all seems so foreign and unreal.
It doesn't matter how good you feel.
You are now to be treated medically,
and you have lost your identity.
You are now "the MI in room 280."

Noise

Noise—clicks, purrs, thumps, beeps, chirps, buzzes.
Normal sounds, alarm sounds.
The quiet sounds, always sounds—
the noise of the Intensive Care Unit.
Gasses hiss; IV fluids drip.
Air pumps buzz; phones ring.
Computers click; keyboards clatter.
Pneumatic tubes thump and crash.
Voices ring, whisper, shout, cry.
Orders are barked, copied, done.
The hustle and bustle of life on the edge
ebbing, flowing, coming and going,
the dance of life and of death,
the everyday chaos of life in the ICU.

Waiting

As nurses it seems to be our fate
to play the game of hurry up and wait.
We receive physician orders for a new med,
but the pharmacist must be in bed.

We call for a respiratory treatment,
but the therapist keeps it a secret.
We call the lab for a STAT blood draw,
but they find an order flaw.

Our doctors want these things done STAT,
but our patients act like brats.
They don't listen to us and call for help,
so then we hear a loud, startled yelp.

They tried to get up out of bed,
got all tangled up, and landed on their head.
So now we need a STAT CT scan,
but that's not in radiology's plan.

So here we sit, waiting for help again.
It really rubs against the grain.
I don't know whether to laugh or curse,
but that's just the life of a nurse.

The Full Monty

I work at the hospital in the ICU—
Intensive Care Unit. It's what I do.
But I have come to know the secret,
and it happens all too frequently.

It's our wonderful gowns that earned our name.
Our hospital gowns are fully to blame.
Our patients don't seem to have a clue
why the nurses laugh and say *I see you.*

If they really knew why I laugh like a loon
when they get out of bed and flash a full moon,
they would get the joke that makes me jaunty
and be really glad it's not the full monty.

Why Did I Become a Nurse?

Why did I become a nurse?
It has always caused me to wonder.
There are jobs that I have done that were worse,
and I made many job blunders.

But being a nurse in the job that I love
Most every day brings me pleasure.
I fit this job like a hand in a rubber glove,
and in it I find a hidden treasure.

But along with the joy, there is also pain.
No matter our efforts, our patients expire,
and sometimes it's hard to explain
when their condition did not seem so dire.

The ones who should live, they die all too soon,
and the ones who should die walk out on their own.
We try to keep our hearts immune
to the pain caused when the spirit has flown.

As a nurse I can only do so much,
and medicine has only so many miracles.
I hope that by my healing touch,
something passes between us that is spiritual.

Friends

She lies awake in a bed strange to her,
surrounded by machines and lights
that add to her confusion and fear
through the lonely hours of a hospital night.

All her life, she's been independent and strong,
but now she feels lost, alone, and weak,
waiting for answers to what is wrong,
and the hours seem to stretch and creep.

I see the fear and strain on her face
as I make my rounds as I can.
Though I am busy, I slow my pace
to sit, talk, and hold a frightened hand.

We speak of her family and life of late,
conversation to help the lonely hours go.
Strangers brought together by a twist of fate
become friends in the blue-green glow

of the monitor and IV pump's dim gleam.
A patient and her nurse pass the time away
until sleep can find her and let her dream
as I quietly slip back to my day.

Hours

The hour from 6 to 7 a.m. is the longest of the day.
We wait for our relief but never know when they
will wander in with coffee cup in hand
to take up where we left off with patients who demand
their breakfast meal delivered to their bed,
then tell us to leave until after they've been fed.
But night nurses, we really couldn't care less.
We are all so tired that I must confess
I agree with my patients; I want to be alone.
After twelve hours of this stuff, I just want to go home.

Death Came to Call

The nursing home is busy,
not enough staff to make the rounds.
With all the noise and confusion,
it's no wonder we miss the sounds—

the sounds of someone crying
from loneliness and pain,
the sounds of a life passing
with nothing left to gain.

We never heard the last sound,
so noisy was the hall.
We never heard him passing
when finally death came to call.

Cowboy

The old man was a cowboy by trade.
Seventy years he rode in the saddle he made.
No wife, no child does he leave here to mourn.
The hour of his passing was eighty-three years since he was born.
He lived out his life with a cowboy's pride,
and now is the time for that one last ride.
He faces the end of this long, lonely trail,
alone here again as he crosses the veil.
The stories he could tell—but there is no one to hear
the good times, the bad times, the rides far and near,
the horses, the cattle, the dogs that he loved,
the work that he did, and the life that he lived.
I was his nurse and sat by his side
to hold his old hand and grieve as he died.
I went to his funeral; he was decked out so fine,
lying in his Sunday best in that white box of pine.
We laid him to rest beneath the grass so green,
just the preacher and me, no one else to be seen.
I stop by, time to time, to visit him there,
just to say hi and offer up a short prayer:
Hope the horses are gentle, the grass green up in heaven.
I can hear you and your pards having a good bull session.
Hope the days are all warm and the skies are all blue
and the nights full of stars as I bid you adieu.

The Forgotten Ones

They are the forgotten ones
who have lived beyond their years,
raised families and children,
shared triumph and tears.

They fought their battles bravely,
and we owe them all our best.
They helped keep our country strong,
toiled away their youth, and now deserve to rest.

But they lie forgotten here
by family and even friends.
They pass their last remaining years
waiting for their lives to end.

We are a people who forget.
We forget
    the ones who need us most,
    the things that they have done,
    and we never know what is lost
    about their wisdom,
    the stories they could tell,
    that they are our family,
    and that we too will grow old.

They Come Together

They come together
    from near and far.
They come and gather
    by plane and by car.
Their voices are soft;
    their movements are slow.
They seem to be lost
    in the room's soft glow.
They are the family
    and the friends
caught up in the gravity
    as life nears its end.
They gather one last time
    to share grief and love,
to say good-bye for all time
    to the one whom they love.

To Be a Nurse

To be a nurse,
    you must be courageous.
It's just our curse
    that you are contagious.
We use standard precautions
    and glove up every time,
just to be cautious
    as we clean up your grime.
We never become complacent
    or let our guard down.
When we care for our patient,
    we wear that cover gown,
because what you might catch
    may not be curable,
and that little scratch
    will lead to something terrible.
So next time you see nurses,
    thank them for their affinity
to a job that could be worse,
    but stay out of their vicinity.

Trauma Team

Trauma team alert, five minutes, trauma red—
The call comes out loud overhead.
The members of the team rush to gather.
The trauma room fills with people who'd rather
be anyplace but here for the arrival
of the patient who relies on us for survival.
We don our armor, lead aprons and cover gowns
that add to our backs at least twenty pounds.
The room turns to a sea of ceil blue
as we begin the dance that we know how to do.
It's choreographed by the patients themselves,
but we are a team who knows how to dance.
We practice our craft at every chance.
The doctors bark out the cadence—
CBC, CMP, PT-INR, CXR, large-bore IV, for the patient.
To anyone watching, they seem mortified,
but all of us are harmonized.
Fifteen minutes at most, surgery awaits.
What seems like chaos falls into place,
and we are left to finish the race.
Covered in blood, sweat, and fears, we stand tired,
exhausted by all that's transpired.
We clean up all the blood and the grime
so we are all ready for the next time
the call comes out overhead—
Trauma team alert, incoming trauma red.

We See You at Your Worst

We see you at your worst
and never see the rest.
We offer strength when you are weak
and never expect yours when we are down.
We will wipe your brow and tears,
and we expect nothing in return.
If we are at our best and do our job well,
we may never see you again.
We will fade from your memory
as we fade from your side,
yet many of you will live in our memories forever.

Your Nurse Is Always Right

When we answer your light
and you should be sleeping
late in the night
when the hours are creeping,
you're becoming confused.
You forget where you're at,
and we're not amused
when you wind up flat
on your back on the floor
because our charting is doubled
and it's quite a chore
and no end of trouble.
So think before you act.
It's only polite.
And remember the fact that
your nurse is always right.

This Old Man

Who is this old man who could one day be me?
What dreams does he have? What visions does he see?
He mumbles and cries out in his sleep as
he talks to friends long gone.
What places has he been to? What things has he done?

In the care of many strangers, he lies now in a hospital bed.
Tubes and wires surround him. They say he's out of his head.
The doctors call it a stroke or maybe a heart attack,
renal insufficiency, diabetes, delirium—but is there any way back

to the person he used to be, to the man
who was loved and respected?
Or is this a one-way track to decline slowly and be rejected
by the family he has raised, by the world he has known,
by society and old friends? For none of them have ever shown

that this man who lies here even enters into their thoughts.
He is caught up in the middle of the medical help he sought.
He came to us for help and care, but his suffering we prolong.
He will never go home now, but is this where he belongs?

He has lived a full life, they say. He has tallied up the score.
It is time for him to die now. His family comes no more.
He lies alone at night now. His mind wanders where it will.
He sleeps the sleep of drugs, thanks to our little pills.

And in these last few hours, I wonder what he sees,
man who lies here dreaming, this old man who could be me.

46

About the Author

Paul Phelps is a registered nurse for Banner Staffing Services in Greeley, Colorado. He works at McKee Medical Center in Loveland, Colorado. He spends most of his hours in the ICU or Emergency Department. He has been a nurse for ten years and has worked for Banner Health for twenty-three years now. He makes his home in Greeley for eight months a year and spends his winters in Port St. Joe, Florida.